JACKSON BROWNSPOT

ISBN 978-1-68526-515-1 (Paperback)
ISBN 978-1-68526-516-8 (Digital)

Covenant Books
11661 Hwy 707
Murrells Inlet, SC 29576
www.covenantbooks.com

JACKSON BROWNSPOT

Catherine Louise

Down around the campground,
There winds a sandy trail.
A creature is running along,
Blond and spotted, with a colored tail.

With joy it approaches.
It's a dog, and he is dear.
With soft brown-spotted ears,
He is coming near.

Anna Marie sits in the sun.
She is cooking by the fire,
Offering food to the dog,
His most earthly desire.

"Hello, you spry dog,
With the brown-spotted ears.
What is your name, please?
I would love to hear."

5

"Greetings, friendly neighbor.
Of course, you may know.
I am Jackson Brownspot,
But now I must go."

"I'm in a hurry.
It's an important date.
If I don't keep moving,
I will surely be late."

Ines with her shears
Is pruning a bush.
He sniffs her cut roses
And keeps trotting on...mush!

"I'm on my way, Ines.
The mass starts now.
My priest is expecting us
To kneel and bow."

Grandpa Pasquale
Is playing bocce ball.
He sees Brownspot passing
And invites the dog.

"Can't stop now, Pasquale,
Not even to play.
To church I must run.
It's my very first day."

Coach Paula is out.
She sees the dog in a hurry.
She waves with a smile.
She has no reason to worry.

"God waits for me, Paula.
Can you hear His call?
I will proudly sing for us
Blessings for all."

It's a beautiful morning,
And he finds his way.
The brown-spotted dog
Has arrived to pray.

"Hello, everyone.
With no pause or delay,
I made it on time,
And I'm here to stay."

A choir of kitties is waiting inside.
Some are dark and some are fair.
He quickly joins them to sing along.
Brownspot gets the last empty chair.

He is here for God,
Receiving gospel and cheer,
Keeping holy his soul,
As Jesus is near.

Ponder and Wonder

God   Relationship   Faith   Blessings

1. Describe Jackson Brownspot to another person.
2. What is most important to Brownspot this morning? Why?
3. List the four campers whom Jackson Brownspot sees on his way to mass.
4. Use your own words and explain what is happening in this story.
5. Suppose you go to church with Brownspot one Sunday. What would you choose to do to be of service?
6. Imagine going camping in Brownspot's campground. Say what you would like to do.
7. Plan for a meeting with Brownspot. Create questions you would like to ask him.
8. How do you prioritize God in your life, and how do you express your faith?
9. Compare living at your home with living in a campground like Brownspot.
10. Predict what blessings are in store and what may happen for Brownspot next.

About the Author

Catherine Louise has been writing as a hobby for several years. Undoubtedly, the power that God has to act for our good has been seen, and so she stresses the importance of having a relationship with God at an early age if you do choose to have one and the difference it makes positively in each of our paths. Catherine is a single mother of two boys, ages ten and four. Both are four-legged, rescued, and adored fur babies from the streets, one of them being Brownspot. Now in Myrtle Beach, South Carolina, they are resident campers and have been living in a fifth wheel, campground hopping for the last four years through the Carolinas.